PIECES OF ANJIE:
POETRY FROM MY SOUL

BY

ANJETTA (ANJIE) WILLIAMS-BROWN

CRAIG GIRLS PUBLISHING

CLARKSVILLE, TENNESSEE

ANJETTA (ANJIE) WILLIAMS-BROWN

COPYRIGHT

Pieces of Anjie: Poetry from My Soul
© 2022 First Edition
© 2025 Second Edition

All rights reserved. No part of this book may be reproduced or transmitted in any form by any means, electronic or mechanical, without permission in writing from the publisher, except by a reviewer who may quote brief passages.

Craig Girls Publishing
Clarksville, Tennessee

Library of Congress Control Number: 2025920508
ISBN: 979-8-218-81006-1

Second Edition

PREFACE

Pieces of Anjie: Poetry from My Soul was written for every person who's had to smile through the storm, search for light in dark places, or needed a reminder that broken pieces can still reflect beauty.

Each poem carries a piece of my story, a whisper of

pain, a spark of faith, and a song of resilience.

My hope is that my poetry is not just words -but healing, ministry, life spoken out loud. I hope each verse is a gift from my soul to yours

DEDICATION

This book is first and foremost dedicated to the Lord above. Without the talent for words, He gave me, this book would not be possible. I am most appreciative to my husband, Darryl, and my family for encouraging me. My dear accomplished screen writer and published cousin, Artemis Craig. Without her publication insight, encouragement, and her publishing bloopers they would have become our publication bloopers. The SoulFire Poetry group helped my growth, my presentation skills, and writing skills. Poet Laureates Henry L. Jones and Chyrel J. Jackson coxed and mentored me along my publication journey,

FOREWORD

Flame Thrower

By Artemis Craig

With her words, she ignites the

soul's fire,

Burning with truth that will embolden and

inspire

She brings comfort to those whose hearts

need to heal,

Her gift is to share the sorrows that others   feel.

Her voice, a torch passed from the ancestors

Chiseled from resilience into a rhythm,

Framing memory into a nation's anthem.

She is the torch bearer striking a flame

Against injustice and the walls of forgetfulness,

Bringing to mind past victories and

hard-fought success.

Her pen draws a fiery trail of bitter tears

that recreate

Moments where dreams were shattered,

and lives were lost,

She dares not remain silent, no matter the cost.

But must speak the truth from her depths,

Her soul laid bare,

Anjie willingly reveals the secrets hidden there.

ANJETTA (ANJIE) WILLIAMS-BROWN

Like a flame thrower set on high,

Her words are superlative and will never die

PIECES OF ANJIE

TABLE OF CONTENTS

LOVE IS IN THE AIR

1. Our Love
2. What's Love Got To Do With It
3. Hugs and Kisses
4. Love Is

FAMILY LOVE

5. The Color of Courage is You
6. The True Value of Blood
7. Mom I Love You
8. What You Mean to Me
9. Dorothy, I Love You
10. Ninety
11. Blessed and Highly Favored
12. Ain't Got No Where to Go
13. The Virtuous Woman
14. A Grandmother's Prayer
15. Red Ink of The Soul
16. Peachy Blessed Day

INSPIRATION

17. I Am Not Far Away
18. Like a Phoenix
19. Mary's Song
20. Faith
21. To Thine Own Self Be True
22. Purpose

JUST FOR FUN

23. Brave Words, Bright Hearts
24. The Flight of the Harpy
25. Up, Up, and Away
26. Cool Breeze Flowing Through the Trees
27. Spring
28. Snow Flakes
29. The Tongue and Me
30. Unbridled Beauty
31. Family Photos

ANJETTA (ANJIE) WILLIAMS-BROWN

4 Love is patient, love is kind. It does not envy, it does not boast, it is not proud.

1 Corinthians 13:4

OUR LOVE

Your love is as breathtaking as the sunset.

Your touch is as tender as a mother's love.

With the peace of Christ ruling your heart,

you are an exceptional man.

I appreciate you.

Two hearts are always better than one,

We will always lift each other up

You will always be there to warm my heart.

I love you.

We shall always keep God in our lives.

He will guard our hearts and our minds.

Whither thou goest I shall go also.

I am eternally yours.

Love is patient.

Love is kind.

Love bears all things.

Together we can endure anything through Christ.

§ 2 §

WHAT'S LOVE GOT TO DO WITH IT

When the lights are out

And the cupboard is bare

What's love got to do with it?

When my heart is low

And nowhere to go

What's love got to do with it

When the wind is cold, and the

house is too

WHAT'S LOVE GOT TO DO WITH IT?

Love is feeding my soul

As well as my stomach

Love is lighting up my life

As well as my dwelling

Love is warming me mentally

As well as physically

Love is making my lips smile

As well as my imagination

LOVE HAS EVERYTHING

TO DO WITH IT

AND NOTHING TO DO WITH IT AT ALL!

§ 3 §

HUGS AND KISSES
Dedicated to my loving Husband

You are the love of my life.
My knight in shining armor.
My protector.
You make me smile when I'm blue.

I look forward to spending

the rest of my life with you.

I'm glad I waited all these years,

for God to place you in my life.

Man of God.

I look back at all the things

I could have been doing.

And all the place I could have gone.

But none of them would have

brought us together.

Let's make it last,

Loving man of mine.

What God has put together,

Let no man pull apart.

Hugs and kisses love of my life

ANJETTA (ANJIE) WILLIAMS-BROWN

§ 4 §

LOVE IS……….

Love is patient, love is kind,

It does not envy, it does not boast,

it is not proud

We are the wind beneath each other's

wings.

It does not dishonor each other,

it is not self-seeking

That is why we will always be as one.

It is not easily angered,

It keeps no record of wrongs.

Forgiveness keeps the love going

strong

Love does not delight in evil,

But rejoices with the truth.

Truth is the rock that keeps

us anchored in each other.

It always protects, always trusts,

Always hopes always perseveres,

Love never fails.

Many things will pass away

but our love will prevail

FAMILY LOVE

DEUTERONOMY 6:6-7

6 And these words that I command you today shall be on your heart. 7 You shall teach them diligently to your children, and shall talk of them when you sit in your house, and when you walk by the way, and when you lie down, and when you rise.

ANJETTA (ANJIE) WILLIAMS-BROWN

§ 5 §

THE COLOR OF COURAGE IS YOU

Dedicated to my six awsome grandkids

You stand tall

Shoulders back

Waiting for what comes

your way

You show no fear!!

You stand tall

Feet planted firm

Waiting for all satan has to

throw your way.

You show no fear!!!

You stand tall

Full coat of armor on

Waiting for anything not of God

Ready to strike cause you know

God's got you

YOU SHOW NO FEAR!!!!!

§ 6 §

THE TRUE VALUE OF BLOOD

Dedicated to my Sister Cousin Artemis Craig

When we were kids we were

always together

We thought we were like Lavern

and Shirley

Making our dreams come true

Doing it our way

We went our separate ways to

do it our way

We had our share of pain

and sorrows

The one thing that we

always held close

And dear was the true value of blood

The blood that kept us close

through thick and thin

Near or far

Happy or sad

When one bleeds with pain

The other bandages with truth

The truth that defines

The true value

of our sister cousin blood

MOM, I LOVE YOU

I can see the twinkling stars in your eyes
I can feel the warmth of the sun in your smile
I can hear the calmness of the wind in your voice
Mom, I love you.

I remember you making all my pain go

away with your kisses
I remember how safe I felt when you hugged me
I remember the Bible stories you told me
Mom, I love you

I've not always acted like the child you raised
I've not always showed you my love
But you've always been the light of my life
Mom, I love you

When I am down you love me
When I am up you love me
You're my friend through thick and thin
Mom, thank you for loving me!

§ 8 §

WHAT YOU MEAN TO ME

Forever rescuing me,

You are my hero.

Always there to protect me,

Thank you.

Together we've had so much fun.

I miss you.

Hope, happiness, and humility

was your motto.

Every day I think of all you've

done for me.

Remembering days pass

comfort, me.

Since you've been gone,

I appreciate you more.

Dad you're the best.

Awesome is the only

word to describe you.

You will forever live in my heart.

ANJETTA (ANJIE) WILLIAMS-BROWN

DOROTHY, I LOVE YOU

Darling, I love you for loving me.

I will never stop.

Only you will love me when I'm good

and when I'm bad, please never change

Remembering all your teachings and

scolding has helped me though 65 years

Open hearted and open arms you've

always had, please never take them away

Tender yet strong is what you taught me.

I'll always be that way.

Heaven has smiled on you lovingly for 94

God filled years, may I receive that same blessing

You are my love, my inspiration, my all.

May God keep you with me for a long, long time.

PIECES OF ANJIE

§ 10 §

NINETY

Nurturing and loving yet

Impeccably poised

Never boastful or judgmental but

Ever so gentle and caring

There is no one like you

You are my sunshine

BLESSED AND HIGLY FAVORED

With the glow of the Angels surrounding you,

You walk in God's footsteps,

You are covered by His feathers,

Under His wings you find refuge,

You are Blessed and Highly Favored.

You dwell in the shelter of the Highest, and

rest in the shadow of the Almighty.

In all your ways you've acknowledged Him, and

He has always directed your path.

You are Blessed and Highly Favored

With the belt of truth and the sword of the Spirit,

you are a Spiritual Mother to all who seek you.

With the shield of faith and shoes of readiness,

you give hope to all the lives you touch.

Yes, you are Blessed and Highly Favored.

"Blessed is she who has believed that what

the Lord has said, to her will be accomplished!"

Dear, you are truly God's Precious Jewel,

one that has the highest value, love and sacrifice.

You are and always will be,

Blessed and Highly Favored.

PIECES OF ANJIE

§ 12 §

AIN'T GOT NOWHERE TO GO

Sit'n on the fence,

Listening to that ole train horn blow.

Wish I was on it,

But ain't got nowhere to go.

The man done sold the place,

My lovely home is gone.

Mama don't seem worried,

But we ain't got nowhere to go.

Mama's cleaning the ole house up,

The place I use to sleep.

Keep ask'n were we gonna go.

She jes keep say'n God'll

show up, He'll make a way.

Sho, hope He hurries,

Cause we still ain't got nowhere to go.

It's almost dark and what do I see,

God com'n down the street,

Look'n like Mr. Tarrant and his

mule Dee

Com'n to get mama and me.

Mama was right, God showed

up on time,

Now, got somewhere to go for

mama and me.

THE VIRTUOUS WOMAN

Your hands have calluses,

You have corns on your feet,

Your body is torn and worn,

And yet, you never complain.

You are always there when needed,

Through good times and bad,

Right or wrong,

And yet you never complain.

Your life has been frazzled and worn,

Most of your dreams are still dreams,

But you've made other's dreams a reality,

And yet, you never complain.

You will never have to worry,

Your teachings will forever live inside of me,

One day I will have to step into your shoes,

And I, will not complain.

§ 14 §

A GRANDMOTHER'S PRAYER

Sit'n here rocking in dis ole chair
Rock'n, rock'n my blues away!!
Lawd I needs to talk to you.
Lawd, Lawd hear my plea
I needs thee

These ole bones is tied
Tied, weary and worn
Can't go another step
I am in need of yo help

What I'm gonna do
Where I'm gonna go
All these here bills is due
I'm depending on you!!!

Father, Father!!!
I stretch my hands to you
Heal them up cause I got much work to do
I lift my eyes to the hills
Help me see a brighter day
I got yo work to do and I can't see
my way

3I praise you Father
Coz you my hope
You my every thang
I see you carry'n me cross
Cross the dangerous seas
And Lawd, Lawd
When I've done all, I can do
I jes want to come home
, come home to see you

ANJETTA (ANJIE) WILLIAMS-BROWN

§ 15 §

Red Ink of the Soul

-Dedicated to my sister cousin Artemis Craig

Always near when we are far

The magic that the red ink brings keeps

our souls as one

It fills the crevasses

And the holes life created

It bandages the bleeding crevasses

of life

No matter far or near

It's the red ink that blots out jealousy

But creates love and devotion

It is the red ink that created

The true value of blood

Between you and I sister cousin Artemis

INSPIRATION

PSALMS 27: 14

Wait on the LORD: be of good courage, and He shall strengthen thine heart: wait, I say, on the LORD

ANJETTA (ANJIE) WILLIAMS-BROWN

§ 16 §
PEACHY BLESSED DAY

When I wake up in the morning,
And smell the honeysuckle as it creeps
Gently across the meadow,
I know that God's Angel Mercy's tender
touch once again
Lovingly and gently woke me up
It is going to be a peachy blessed day!

When I hear the rhythmic thump of the rain
on the ole tin roof.
And see the monstrous winds, tossing
Huge trees to and fro all around me
I know that God's Angel Goodness has
once again protected me
It is going to be a Peachy Blessed Day!

When life's walls start closing in around me,
And satan is knocking at every door,
and climbing through   the windows too
I know that God's Angel Peace has once
again, comforted me.
It's going to be a Peachy Blessed Day!

I know that if God brought me to the mountain
He will guide me through the mountain
I know that nothing is impossible for my God
I know that God has worked out all my problems

While I am still thinking about them
I know that He is and awesome God,
And that is why, it is always going to be a
PEACHY BLESSED DAY!

§ 17 §

I'M NOT FAR AWAY
Dedicated to those who have lost a loved one

Though I'm not with you,
I'll always be near.
I'll be wherever you are,
I'll be with you in truth and spirit.

When you want to see me,
Just lift your eyes to the sky.
When you want to hear me,
Just listen to your heart.
As often as you share your kindness,
That's how often you'll feel me close to you.

You'll never be alone,
For I'll always comfort you.
You'll never be friendless,
For I'm your best friend.
You'll never be in need,
For I'll always care for you.

Though I'm not with you,
I'm not far away.
I'm gone to stay with the Father,
I'm gone to be with the King.

Cheer-up be of good courage,
I've walked a long road and fought a hard battle.
Let not your heart be full of sorrow,
For I'm not gone to stay.
My departure is only for a short while,
I'll be back some day.

I've walked a long road and fought
a hard battle.
Let not your heart be full of sorrow,
For I'm not gone to stay.
My departure is only for a short while,
I'll be back some day.

LIKE A PHOENIX

Like a Phoenix I rise when

least expected,

I erupt through the volcanic ash with

a falcon's speed!

Wings glowing with embers of amber, reds and oranges,

Unsinged! Unscathed! Unstoppable!

With the eyes of an eagle,

The cunning of a fox,

But like a Phoenix I rise from the dead,

Reborn, renewed, and better than before!

Catch me if you can,

You can't kill me,

Try to keep me down.

Like a Phoenix I'll always rise again

PIECES OF ANJIE

§ 19 §

MARY'S SONG

Lord, you gave me a blessing

You said it was your prized possession

One that would save the world

You gave me your son

Your Angels Goodness and Mercy gave me the news

Early one crisp sunny morning

They told me not to worry,

For you gave me your son

The neighbors are starting to whisper

Everyone has and opinion

But your blessing no one has mention

I know it is a great task I have

Being the mother of the Savior

But God will Guide me

For He has entrusted me with the King

Glory be to you, my Heavenly Father

I won't let you down

I have your prized possession.

I have your Son

FAITH

I lift my eyes to you.

You're my light and salvation

I hide myself in thee

You are my refuge

I keep your words in my heart,

So that I'll always please you.

You are the wind beneath my wings,

I can soar to endless heights.

You are the beacon in the distance

Guiding me through life

You are my rock, my sword, and shield.

Whom shall, I fear?

With you all things are possible,

You cannot fail.

In you I put all my trust

Your Angels Goodness and Mercy protect me,

You are my God!

§ 21 §

TO THINE OWN SELF BE TRUE

To thine own self be true,

Make sure you know what to do

Never agonize over the situation,

Just remember the rule of truth,

I can do all things through Christ who strengthens me.

To thine own self be true.

Friends may sympathize,

But they can never realize,

Friends can lend a shoulder to cry on,

But they can never really comfort you.

To thine own self be true.

To thine own self be true

True enough to know when you have

done all you can do.

To thine own self be true

True enough to know that there is only

one who can help you

To thine own self be true

True enough to take it to the mountain

and leave it there

ANJETTA (ANJIE) WILLIAMS-BROWN

§ 22 §

PURPOSE

When the sun shines

The world is warm and happy

When the wind blows

The world is wrapped in a blanket of peace

The rose blooms

The world opens in glee

The bees sing melodiously

The world is covered in sweet nectar

The sun sets

The word is blanked in a beautiful glow

All things have a purpose

We must look pass what we see

We must look into our hearts

If only we listen

The whispers will inspire us

The words will always sustain us

If only we listen

PIECES OF ANJIE

§ 23 §

BRAVE WORDS, BRIGHT HEARTS

In an unfamiliar place
A place with no real name
It doesn't look like home
It doesn't feel like home
But it is your new home
Your resilience begins to shine
Like the sunshine brilliant bright
With talented voices,
strong and clear
Your words tell a loud story
Your words show strength
Your words show determination
Your words show you are not the
sum of your surroundings
You are not victims
You are survivors
You are not followers

You are leaders
You are the foundation of tomorrow
Never let your smiles fade
For then the sun will lose its shine

Never let your words disappear
For then the wind will cease to blow
Never lose your words For the clouds will
forever cry

You carry in you the strength of 1000 lions
The determination of a cheetah
And a heart and soul that spells love.
Keep your head to the sky
A brighter day is ahead.

[12] "Six days do your work, but on the seventh day do not work, so that your ox and your donkey may rest, and so that the slave born in your household and the foreigner living among you may be refreshed.

EXODUS 20:9-11

§ 24 §

THE FLIGHT OF THE HARPY

He stands majestically
He is massive
He is powerful
He loves to soar high in the sky

South American rainforest is one of his hangouts
He can see all from his perch
He spreads his 6 feet wings
Fixes his gaze
He sees his food
In the sky
On the ground

He takes off like a jet
Gliding higher and higher
He can ascend almost to the heavens
He is a bird of prey

Ascending to heights higher than imagined
Soaring 600 feet in the air
Gliding relaxed and reserved
He is one with the 'wind
Ascending higher
Scouting for prey
Talons poised
Wings still
No bird is safe

God's creation is awesome
He made the Harpy
Massive,
Yet agile,
Watching his ascent into the sky
My imagination ascends with him

ANJETTA (ANJIE) WILLIAMS-BROWN

UP UP AND AWAY

Up, Up and away

In my beautiful balloon

Soaring high in the sky

Higher and Higher

I feel free

Gliding smoothly over the ocean

The sun plays with the yellow color

of the balloon

The tulips relax snuggly

High above the mountains

The beautiful white snow caps

As the fog rises from the water

It gives off a beautify bluish hue

The blue sky caresses the landscape

Bringing everything together as one

The heat propels us higher

As the wind carries

I feel like a bird soring

Ascending freely

Mentally free…..

Mentally free

§ 26 §

COOL BREEZE FLOWING THROUGH THE TREES

Leisurely strolling, absorbing the vast array of hues,
The crimsons, bricks, rose, tangerines, shades of violets,
Inhaling the delicious aroma of flowers lingering
on the forest floor,
The captivating sells of the stargazer lilies, the delicate
smell of the primrose,
The sweet smell of the honeysuckle wraps gently around
my head like a Christmas wreath,
Each fragrance playing and dancing with the atmosphere,

The melodious harmony of the forest families at play
and work,
Papa squirrel busy gathering nuts,
Mama squirrel tentatively watching the twins,
The forest is alive getting ready for their Father Winter's
sleep,

The waterfall's glassy water filled with prisms,
Gently bounce and splash,
As it drizzles across the rocks calmingly,
The lily pads and the lotus blossoms lay lazily on the
water surface,
Enjoying an afternoon chat,

The hot air balloons hang in the air like chandeliers,
They look like droplets of rainbow color ink,
Slowly gliding down the walls of the sky,

The cool wind whispers sweet nothings in my ear,
Tenderly telling me Autumn is here!

As the blankets of snow roll away
And the lake waters thaw
And the crisp winds turn warm
The air fills with the aroma of life in its infancy

As the warm winds blow
The lilacs and foxgloves play laughingly
The hyacinth opens their arms
welcoming the bees tender kiss
It's spring and life is beautiful

The mountains in the distance glow luscious reds
the sunset is tranquil and exhilarating
Spring is ….. intoxicating!!!!!!!!!!!!!!!!!
Spring is …… exhilarating!!!!!!!!!!!!!!!!!
Spring is ……. imagination!!!!!!!!!!!!!!!!

Spring is…………!!!!!!!!!

PIECES OF ANJIE

§ 28 §

Snowflakes

Little lint like flakes touch me

Brushing my face like a feather

My body felt like it had just

had a cool burst of peppermint

As the cool breeze accompanying the

flakes playing back and forth

It makes my mind flow free

in the breeze

The trees are wrapped snuggly

in the snow

The reflection of the sun makes a

brilliant white star like light

As it blankets the ground

like a white fluffy rug

Only God can create something

so beautiful

Only God.....!!!

ANJETTA (ANJIE) WILLIAMS-BROWN

§ 29 §

THE TONGUE AND ME
A dramatization of Proverb 18:21

Woke up one morning and The Tongue was mad

Don't know why but it was bad

Could have been something that happened

yesterday

Could have been a week or so ago

One thing for sure The Tongue was

Cutthroat

Chainsaw

Woodchipper mad

She started slicing with a double-edged sword

SLASH RIGHT SLASH LEFT

Heads rolled everywhere uphill,

round the corner

The house was destroyed

It is now a house divided

Split in half and split some more

It was Humpy Dumpty broke

Tongue just look and walked away

She knew there was nothing she

could do or say I asked her why

She simply said I got out of control and lost my head.

Unbridled Beauty

She knows no boundaries
Carefree as the wind
Glistening beautifully in living color
Her home is adorned with
Beautiful trees and plants
In a dense wet land

She thrives in unusual places
She can be found on roads
Less traveled
She possesses quiet strength and reliance
She is as beautiful as the morning sun

She stands six (6) feet tall with
A pitcher for a body that's
Filled with luscious juices
Irresistible to all passers by
Once inside, all comfy and relaxed
She closes her doors and you are trapped
Beauty can be deceiving
For the beautiful pitcher plant
Is an extreme carnivore

FAMILY PHOTOS

Mom and 2 of the
5 grandchildren

Mom's 90th surprise
birthday party.

Grandmama at 85

Mom Grand and
Great Grand

Hubby

Mom and
Dad 1993

PIECES OF ANJIE

Anjetta (Anjie) Williams-Brown, recently retired from Tennessee State University (TSU) after serving as Business Coordinator for 22 years. She was the first African American female in Tennessee to pass the Educational Facilities Professional examination; a Facilities Management certification.

She is a 1981 University Alabama Birmingham graduate with a concentration in Medical Records Technology. She is a 2009 Tennessee State University graduate with a concentration in Public Relations and Communications. She has served on various boards and organizations which include: Soul Fire Poetry Group; TSU President's Fellows Program; Past President and Charter President of Toastmasters, Inc.; Past Board Member Women in Higher Education in Tennessee (WHET); Past Board Member Tennessee State University Women's Center.

She self-published her first poetry book entitled "Pieces of Anjie: Poetry from my Soul, December 2022. She currently hosts several poetry platforms. Her hope is to give all poets a chance to share their craft and promote their writings.

She is currently using her poetic words to start a handmade/custom greeting card company, "Pieces of Anjie". She enjoys ...., writing and performing poetry, and spending time with her grandchildren. She is looking forward to publishing a series of inspirational poetry in various mediums.

www.ingramcontent.com/pod-product-compliance
Lightning Source LLC
LaVergne TN
LVHW061334060426
835512LV00017B/2674